Rhymes With Dre is a self-published collection of poems. Words that once lived quietly in my phone now rest in your hands. Hold it gently.

Copyright 2021 © Andrea Cenon

ISBN: 978-0-5788-3037-7
All rights reserved.

RHYMES WITH DRE

Andrea Cenon

to anyone who has ever made me laugh

*and maybe that guy at the grocery store who lit up when I walked in
& demanded that I be in a relationship.*

I wonder if
LA
knew I was gone.
did the palm trees feel
my admiration distance.
were the bougainvilleas
aware it lost a gaze.
maybe traffic
got a minute lighter.
or the heat even warmer,
losing a body to shine on.

—965 miles away

He saw her walking
from a distance.
she was carrying a plant
almost twice her size.
surely towering over her.
the leaves were wilting
and the edges have browned.
as her pace grew quick,
her leaves fell quicker.
finally, she reached Him.
dropping her plant at His feet,
her eyes welling,
she glances up at Him,
only to make sure He's listening
her hands gently caress the
leaves she has left,
with disappointment in her
breath,
she asks,
"do you care?"
His eyes locked towards her,
He responds,
"greatly."

Detrimental that
we are the problem
yet
empowering that
we are the solution.

—humanity

Beauty has been lost
in the game of telephone,
surviving through
what you thought you heard,
beauty is not for you to define,
we do not need to hold it together
by our collective point of view.
beauty does not have to agree with you.
nor us.
beauty is who we need it to be
not who we've told it to become.
it is not captured in perfection,
but suffocated by it.
it is living and demanding of
space to be as it needs to be.
we hold it as it gasps for air,
are we afraid that beauty
is actually not up for discussion,
but something that simply is.
beauty is,
is who we are,
not who we tell it to be.

My hair has a mind of it's own
dark and textured
obedient to a fault
sometimes I wonder what
it would say if it could speak
it knows it's made
for and from the islands
with remnants of an inland country
and colonizers just the same

Sometimes I think
poets are red flags
dipped in milk and honey
whose
words that don't sweat
baby they glisten.
rhythm you can read
from miles away.
handing out
a single stemmed prose
already you're captivated
careful,
it's the eloquence
that comes without warning.

Disappointment
is suffocating.
it steals my air
taking up space
like it never plans
to leave.
it closes in
on what hope I held
and forces me
to choose
whether to
breathe
or hope.

Sometimes
knowing your worth
feels like the sun
on a cloudy day
I know it's there
but is it?

When you walk into the room
and you see the tables are taken
and the chairs are
far from reach
when you walk into the room
and every hand seems to be held
and heads don't turn
and your eyes are unmet
when you walk into the room
and it feels empty.
I hope you remind yourself
that still,
"there is no lack."
and maybe that room isn't yours
to walk into
so keep walking,
until you find the seats and
hands
waiting for you.
there is no lack.
and there's a room
for you.

Rushing home
in clothes that have
collected my sweat
a discomfort I welcomed,
the heat
embraced me
like it missed me,
the sun stared at me blankly
knowing I was a familiar face.
I rode in peace
with an old friend.
when I reached home,
I smelled like the sun.
as my shirt grazed my nose.
suddenly I heard my parents,
after every hug
from a day outside,
they'd always say,
you smell like the sun.
I didn't know
how distant home felt,
until I smelled it so close.

— take me home

I couldn't begin to understand
the fragility of life
the true weight of time,
why sitting in yesterday
felt like an eternity
but in a moment's notice
we are greeted by eternity.
I couldn't begin to understand
the magnitude of this life
it's temporary,
we have today.
Goodbye, **24**
hours, the measure of our days.
I couldn't begin to understand
life.
I am observer
and member.
from where I stand,
I am moved that though we don't truly
know the entirety of our existence,
still we're here,
...

in the face
of pain. of joy,
to persist and seek,
that which we don't fully grasp.
and in it we unravel
the complicated gifts
our days each hold.
from where I stand,
I'm disappointed but grateful
from where I stand,
I look to the Lord
with Whom I'm only able.
from where I stand,
I couldn't begin to understand.
life is only short.
so as life goes without regard,
our only response
is that we must live
and live fully.

—kobe

I'm friends with the girl in the castle.
her friendship felt like a fortress
a little enchanted
with tall walls
and a bridge to cross.
it felt safe with mystery always to uncover.
we roamed freely,
joy kept us company,
time flew and still I'd wonder
who is the girl in the castle.
she held depth
in the palm of her hands,
tethered tightly.
there's always more
to the girl in the castle.

You are living in your thank you speech.
working through your good old days
when trust is your luxury
and hope made your ends meet.
you are in your looking back
when His faithfulness punctuated
every sentence of strength
your days made you write.
you are in it, my friend
but you won't always be.
this is not your forever.
when the morning comes
to the story you're living
it'll be the story you'll tell.
continue on,
and open.
I'll meet you onward.

She's like the warmth
of your tears
rolling down your cheeks.
arriving as if to say
you aren't alone

she feels like
unexpected joy
that persists,
a discovery of
more,
more fries in the bag.

she's like the presence
of fullness
you begin to crave.

her strength
is attractive.

she will catch
you with the
gentleness of her words,
not in knowing you'd fall,
but loving you when you did.

she is present
and that is her gift.

she's like the best
reflection of you.

dark midnight.
cream silk
black coffee.
brown earth
and sand.
white snow
ocean blue
golden flower
different hue.
the sun rises
the sun sets.
the sun shines
just the same
on you
and me.

—in His image

Of all places
God said,
here.
where
I'd try to build
the narrative
already
so beautifully
constructed
in my mind
the once upon a time
of God's faithfulness
and happily ever afters
of
God is good
all the time.
but this narrative
between
mind
and reality
is a war on perfection
i'd never win.
i saw it in my head
and hoped
that when I opened
my eyes
it would.
that it would simply
be.
But hope differed
and expectations unmet
I sat in disbelief
wondering if
disappointment
was the promise land.
where His promises
would never land.
but, God You said
breakthrough.
did You mean
that I'd be broken
through?

as the sun rose
and set
time shuffled
365 days or so
I sit in belief.
I look back in awe
when I wondered
why city of roses,
and he said
"It's the perfect climate
for roses to grow."
petals unto
stem into
meeting myself
today
I've grown.
out of all places,
God said
here
lies out of my
comfort zone.

thank you for
this version of me
I'm meeting today.
in-the-perfectly
in-process,
grace-is-not-earned,
you-are-enough,
dream-even-bigger,
keep-your-wonder-
close,
let-life-build-your-faith,
look-to-Him,
author
perfecter.
of all places,
God said
here.

His smile
grabbed me
by the waist.
pulled me in
close
enough,
he only
needed to whisper.
his words replayed
like Summer radio.
his existence
was addicting.

She asked if
I still thought about him
like he was a library book
I forgot to return.
is there a place to drop off
these thoughts?
maybe a goodwill
accepting unfinished words,
interrupted affection,
run on sentences
that form
my version of him.
if so, drop the addy
so I can let go of this
past due zaddy.

— i'll pay the fiooone

These memories of you
that I'd hope I'd forget by now
the pop up ads of you
acting as figment connections
random and unwelcomed
reminding me that you
existed...
as if I'd forgotten

The innocent strangers
now unfortunate reflections of you
familiarities that make me wonder.

I'm unlearning you
exiting these incessant reminders
I walk the opposite direction
of the feelings I had

I'm unlearning you
disassociating joy with your words
forgetting that you
didn't create laughter,
I'm unlearning you
...

rewiring my mind
to let go of these inside jokes,
that when I turn to drop the punchline
my memories expect you to catch,
I remember my no to you.
a yes to me, my worth.

trust me, I look forward
to the days
when these pop up ads
no longer pop up and add
to the clutter that is you.
when a guy with a beard
is just an innocent stranger.
not the trigger in my heart,
"is that him?"

but I gave you time,
so it's only fair to give myself the same.
I'm unlearning you.

Subtly, I held expectation.
subtly, I waited.
subtly, I welcomed you in.
I opened the door to maybe.
I let you sit in hopefully.
I spent time with what if.
subtly, it came.
subtly, it went.
subtly, disappointment lingers.
because again,
I met hello
and
goodbye.

—friend zone

I keep seeing
my favorite parts
of me
in walking reflections
of he's not the one

but I like the way
he dances to
the rhythm that
I always hear

and I like the way
he smiles
at me like
I hold a safe place

but I also like the way
he speaks
his words
woven and
strung with a depth
only his voice knows

I like the way
his existence
reminds me of possibility,
anything can happen

but I don't like the way
they weren't here to stay.

—to all of em'

She held her pain
where she once held his love.
waiting for forgiveness
to feel less like betrayal,
tears paved a road
leading to memories
they'd made.
what if's
crept like paper cuts,
whispers to turn back
tug at her heart,
but against the comfort
of knowing
she kept going
at the pace of
discovery.
unlocking her
more than he ever sought to,
she found herself
on a tears paved road.
wanted,
she always was,
she sat
in hopes of stillness
breathing to the beat of
her own heart.
rhythm she's always heard
...

but sometimes muted.
turn the volume up
in this world
without him,
a world where ache
held hands
with hope
the same way night and morning
intertwine,
it wasn't set in stone
but written and rewritten.
a back and forth
of all the versions of
herself that existed
laying bare
to see
far more worthy than
he'd ever let on.
she's healing.
so she holds this pain,
steps ahead
of when it used to hold her
but her hands won't hold it forever.
she's healing.

I think adventure means
it is far from home
running with
holding hands with
in search of,
sometimes lonely
and often missing
others
I hold dearly.
I think adventure
is riddled with choices
and second guesses
and wrong turns
and disappointments.
well, damn
this is hard.
it lures hope
and pain just the same.
adventure is not where I'm from
it takes place in
more than once upon a time
in lands past the mountains,
where are the palm trees?
guaranteed with new
friends and opposition
easy it's not
...

pain free it's not,
but it is radically onward,
an exercise in adventure
where my heart carries
and picks up,
it clings to home
without the comfort of it
it tethers my heart to depth
but wades by the shallows,
I look around and
see nothing familiar.
everything is untouched
and it is both exciting
and heart breaking.
I'm on an adventure
and I didn't even realize.
I craved this and prayed for it.
I thought adventure
meant something else
when all along
adventure
meant the life
I'm already living.

Does love get away?
is it something that escapes
if we don't hold it correctly?
maybe love doesn't get away
forever,
but for a while
it goes unnoticed
because it shows up differently
than we'd like,
maybe love doesn't get away
but it's taking longer than expected
to come back
like we want.
so, live your life.
grace for your heart
to keep living
when love lingers
but doesn't stay
as long as we'd hope,
grace for our hearts
to stay open
when love comes back around.
because it always does.

She looked at me
like I was made of diamonds.
her eyes lit up
at the simplicity
of my presence.
her excitement
never grew tired
knowing her blood
gave my heart a beat.
I don't understand it,
but I feel it.

— "moe•del," she says.

My memories
are your biggest fan.
I catch her drifting of
to reruns,
sneaking glimpses into
specific episodes that
only show you
as the best we've ever had.
in her world,
I'm the bad guy
and my dear,
you are the good guy.
I reel her back,
but you lure her in
to the past,
telling stories that will
only ever be a rerun.
we are an episode of Friends
we aren't anything new,
we are only old news.
…

she wears
rose-colored
you-can-do-no-wrong-colored
remembers-how-you-smelled-so-good-colored
glasses.
someone get this girl a new prescription
before she starts writing fiction.
my memories hold you fondly
maybe with precious hope,
a double edged sword.
but as the show must go on,
my dear, so will I.

—I was hoping poems would help me get over you

I've met violence
in furious rage
and stillness.
I've met quiet
in fear
and shame.
they held hands,
two faced reflections
I've known dearly.
I've known
these brothers.
this father,
I've known.

For a while
I held them close
to my heart.
chosen brothers
from time
and not birth
I met these walking
men of love and joy.
I clinged tightly
to the comfort of their presence
I laughed daily
because it was a joy
to be.
my eyes lit up
in a different way.
I rested in their friendship
with grace to sink deeply
I felt loved.
and while seasons change,
I'll remember them as
walking men of love and joy.

I wondered if she was tired,
wearing love like a name tag
turning around whenever
someone new called her name.
catching moments
to build forever
only to find it fleeting.

Loosen your grip
on tightly held affection,
feeling
does not hold you captive.
wait and see
that maybe one day
is actually a day
waiting for you.

I'm tired
of half baked
of maybes
of sometimes
of I'll let you know when I know.
I'm tired
of being enjoyed
and not pursued.
I'm tired of
your one foot in and one foot out
until
they decide,
I'm no longer enjoyable
what is it about me,
wait
what is it about you,
that enjoys only
parts of me,
enjoys spending
my time
my energy
my space.
why do you exist in portions?
controlled just enough
to keep me answering
your call when you do
and waiting till you do again.
catch me smiling with relief
when your convenience
finally sends me a message.
don't get me wrong,
I enjoy this.
...

but, do you treat
all your friends like this?
this call-at-night,
this hang-whenever,
this consistently-casual-effort.
I've been told to be open,
give men space,
maybe time to figure things out.
but, it only ever feels like
I'm waiting for you to see,
it only ever feels like
I'm hoping,
hoping you'd learn,
what I already know,
that I'm worth it.
what I'm not is casual,
casually yours and your homie.
I'm intentional,
gotta risk it to get with it type of lady
I'm sorry I can't keep
playing telephone
maybe if we'd met before your walls
or just when we were younger,
maybe our maybe
could've been
who knows
anyways,
I'll see you around.

— to the ones who enjoyed having me around.

Forget all that glitters
let's sit in the backyard
of a quiet life
the peak afternoon sun
is as loud as it gets,
shining like the only
gold we need.
sit away with me
master stillness
like we've mastered its contrast
I'm in no rush.

Tears knew
they weren't welcome,
so they didn't stay.
but occasionally
they'd walk in to say
a little something
in mixed emotions
of the weight
of temporary love,
picked up
and let go,
in the back and forth
of hope,
that fades into eventually
this wouldn't work.
tears never
made themselves
comfortable
like strangers
waiving from a distance,
nodding at our attempt
of interested
but not enough.

I'm afraid that
love is too precious
to hold me.
I'm afraid that
love is as fragile
as I think it to be.
I'm afraid that
love stands at a distance.

—Is love afraid?

If you find that
you've only discovered
me skin deep,
that the most beautiful
thing I've to offer
wrinkles in time,
then you have not seen me.

Her heart has always been held.
but maybe it never felt heard
or seen.
until he walked in
wearing thoughtfulness
and kindness like a uniform.
his words are rhythmic,
sounds her heart have always
danced to.
he walks towards her like
she holds his safe place
she finds herself taken
by his gaze that surrounds her
like a blanket,
she didn't know would feel so safe.
he is tangible
when faith is anything but.
he has arms to catch
and a mind to speak
creating worlds
she could sink into.
so where does a love like this fit?
the kind that reminds the little girl
she's always been worth it.
the kind that is gentle
and present.
where does a love like this fit?
the kind that stays a while.
does a love like this fit?

I hope
you enjoy today.
I hope you
invest in friendships
that feel temporary,
give love a shot
even if it may not last.
I hope today
gets your best.
I hope you
find moments
to fully
sit back
and see
that today is good
that today is enough.
I hope you
enjoy today,
because today
was once your best to come.

Rejection is
getting in a hot car
on a summer day
wearing shorts
with leather seats
not knowing the air conditioning
was broken
only blowing hot air
you open the window
in hopes of relief
but it's heat unto heat
a slow burn.
until you start
moving
and the car
gets going.
in that moment
you're overheated
but cool air finds its way
when you keep going.

He said
he didn't know
how he felt,
like we only happened
in my mind.

—who hurt you?

What if
certainty was
bondage?
The comfort
of control
your prison.

Disrupt me
when I strive
interrupt me
when I forget
steal my gaze
when I'm distracted
remind me
of who I am
remind me
of the beauty of today
remind me
that tomorrow can wait

Tell me why
the comfort
of your existence
is the home
I love coming back to.

—familyiar

The unknown preys
agains our resilience
that hangs on
a restless knowing
there must be more.

— hope

There will be days,
where your faith
at the sight
of living
quivers,
it's knees will bend
and you will lay there,
holding it's fragility
that fell from the
sky of your chest,
and your mind
will wander
pacing back and forth
panicking for answers
at the end of questioning
did God let me down?
again,
because the way your
faith slipped through
your composure,
you lay there,
stunned at the
weight of disappointment.
...

as you wonder through
thoughts outside of grace,
your people,
should you allow them
will soften their stance
to meet you where you lay
reminding you of
everything disappointment wiped
your mind of.
you lay there,
with people holding the fallen parts
of your sadness
that comes at the expense
of living
fully,
they aren't disappointed
in you,
but excited, that though you found
yourself in this moment
questioning tomorrow,
they lay there,
telling you of
Who is only certain of tomorrow.

I didn't know
I could write poems,
till I left
and my words
chased after you

girl,
don't give parts of yourself
in representation of your energy
transactions at the cost of your body,
interaction
that only unravels you,
to someone
who isn't aware
he is unwrapping you.

Loneliness fit like
my favorite jacket
that I've worn
a couple times this week.
I think the familiarity
is the most comforting part.
the certainty
that it'll hold me
when I need it to.
it's easy going
and doesn't ask
too many questions,
loneliness is unassuming
offering itself to catch
the weight of
joy differed.

Our work
is not
solely for our hands
it is not only
from our eyes.
our work needs to live,
they are never
dead on arrival,
it must explore
outside our peripheral.
it doesn't stop
at the point of completion
nor is it only to be bought,
our work needs to
hold doors open,
pour and fill
and multiply
creativity,
outside
off our palms,
our work is to break
the boundaries its put on us.
when it finds life
outside of itself,
then we've not only created,
but we've created well.

I see you
gripping the ocean
in the palms of your hands
the waves are slipping
through your fingers.
unclench your fists
the ocean does
not belong in your grasp.
peace is not fragile.
the same ocean that
roars,
flirts quietly with the sand.
be the ocean
that you hold
so tightly.

"Ang layo ng tingin mo"
my parents would say
or "your gaze is far"
it's true my gaze was distant
a well travelled mind.
even in the same room
my attention stayed miles away
booking flights
that would never take off,
catching myself
watching the good old days
of what was
of what if
of alternate endings.
searching through
versions of myself
I've left behind
building vacant worlds
I've yet to occupy.
distant moments
often caught my eyes
but in a few blinks,
I'm back.

I can't wait
to read this poem
she says.
knowing I run to words
to catch my sighs
this would've been
about one day,
but instead
it's any day.
enjoy your life.
It'll travel often
finding home
in places to stay
and places to leave
finding people
to sink into
and let go of.
you'll see the sun rise
and set.
mountains and valleys
are well acquainted in this life.
you can smile
and feel pain
within moments
blurred together.
...

meeting future versions
of yourself,
fruit of your past
it's not predictable,
but that's a good thing.
your heart will ride
high in hope
sink low in disappointment.
you'll meet resilience
a thousand times 7.
day and night exist mutually.
let it be.
don't distract your way out of living.
this is my poem about life,
life on a Sunday night
where I met myself
brave without pride
bold and steady
a subtle softness
to hold what comes my way
and let it go
when it doesn't choose to stay.

—sunday is one day

I opened the doors
to my promise,
finding
the walls
suffocating me
I haven't stopped
looking for the exit since.
differed and
in search of return
to the unknown
of today,
than the unknown
of tomorrow.
I knew
I couldn't go back.
but maybe,
I could quicken,
checking off the boxes of
today
and
tomorrow.
...

holding my breath
till I found a season
worth breathing in.
then I heard
trust, be still.
I ignored the Voice
hoping He'd change His mind.
But I was silenced,
by His grace,
inescapable I found
myself trapped
in His faithfulness.
so,
the vv I opened
to my promise
were actually
met by the revolution
of walking in grace,
but nothing else.

Who told you
that your body
couldn't drape unto itself,
folding like chocolate
enveloping all that
your body requires,
just because it's said,
doesn't mean it's true.
have you noticed the way velvet dances,
it is inspired by you.
when you turn around
and see that your body
craves more space
then space
you shall give it.
your body is living,
designed outside of perfection,
let it live.
let it move
let your body
roll.
catching waves that only a body
alive and well can.
when you see your body searching,
call it back home,
remind it
that it is already found.

Thoughtfully,
our hearts
were designed
with mixed emotions
in mind.
enough space
to hold loss
and joy.
characteristically
resilient
painfully aware,
it's alive.
finding days worth
breathing in.
feeling,
as you allow.
careful, you're precious.
but just as strong.
wonderfully, be.

My wealth arrives in waves
of i miss you
of when are you moving back
of i just called to say hi
of music they send
of laughter that shakes my core
of language only we speak
of the comfort of our time
of knowing me
of reality checks
of i love you
of you inspire me
of your voice
of thinking of you
of every little thing that exists.

—where the money resides

Thanks for
holding my hand.
seasonal
parts of me
represented
in vacant hands
waiting to be held.
to the sisters in this place
to the brothers in my days,
thanks for holding my hand.
to you I've yet to meet,
after these words,
still
my hands
as doors
wait
for when you'll hold mine.

RHYMES WITH DRE

You've reached the end or flipped
to the back, either way I'm honored.
Did you read the one about you?
These pages have held portions
of my life and others, I hope you
found something to hold onto.
Revisit and reread as you need.
I'll catch you in and out of these pages.

Andrea Cenon

RHYMES WITH DRE

Special Thanks to—

My mom who makes it seems like
I light up her world 24/7.

My dad who is always proud
of anything I do.

My siblings & cousins for making life
feel more full than it
sometimes is.

My best friends who continue to
make life exceedingly, abundantly
more sweet than I could ever
hope it to be.

To everyone who inspired a
poem whether good or bad,
I appreciate you.

Andrea Cenon

www.ingramcontent.com/pod-product-compliance
Ingram Content Group UK Ltd.
Pitfield, Milton Keynes, MK11 3LW, UK
UKHW041301180426
11947UKWH00009B/609